Hallelujah! THE STORY OF LEONARD COHEN

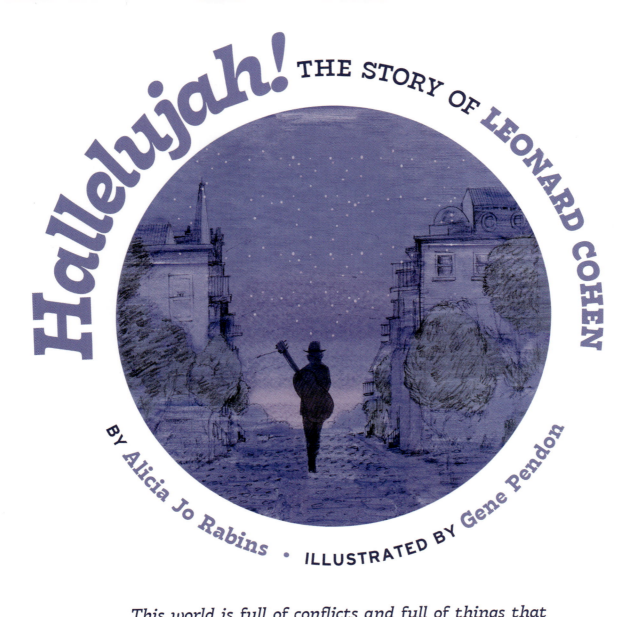

BY Alicia Jo Rabins • ILLUSTRATED BY Gene Pendon

This world is full of conflicts and full of things that cannot be reconciled. But there are moments when we can . . . reconcile and embrace the whole mess, and that's what I mean by "Hallelujah."

—LEONARD COHEN

*For all the lovers of music and workers in song:
past, present, and future.*
— A.J.R.

To the poetic soul that draws from a sincere and authentic place.
— G.P.

Note: Alicia Jo Rabins, this book's author, is also a musician. Leonard Cohen's music has been one of her main inspirations as a songwriter ever since she first heard his songs at summer camp.

This book tells the story of Leonard Cohen's song "Hallelujah." If you aren't familiar with the song, you might want to listen to it! You can find a cover version of "Hallelujah" and other Leonard Cohen songs sung by Alicia at www.aliciajo.com.

Apples & Honey Press
An Imprint of Behrman House Publishers
Millburn, New Jersey 07041
www.applesandhoneypress.com

ISBN 978-1-68115-688-0

Text copyright © 2025 by Alicia Jo Rabins
Illustrations copyright © 2025 by Behrman House

All rights reserved. No part of this publication may be translated, reproduced, stored in a retrieval system or transmitted, in any form or by any means, electronic, mechanical, photocopying, recording or otherwise, for any purpose, without express written permission from the publishers.

Library of Congress Cataloging-in-Publication Data
Names: Rabins, Alicia Jo, author. | Pendon, Gene, illustrator.
Title: Hallelujah : the story of Leonard Cohen / by Alicia Jo Rabins ; illustrated by Gene Pendon.
Description: Millburn, New Jersey : Apples & Honey Press, 2025. | Audience: Ages 5-8 | Audience: Grades K-1 | Summary: "From his childhood in Montreal to his eventual stardom in adulthood, Leonard Cohen looked toward music to express his emotions, spirituality, and impressions of the world around him. The focus is Cohen's masterpiece Hallelujah, his struggles to write it and his perseverance to have it recognized"-- Provided by publisher.
Identifiers: LCCN 2024046857 | ISBN 9781681156880 (hardcover)
Subjects: LCSH: Cohen, Leonard, 1934-2016--Juvenile literature. | Cohen, Leonard, 1934-2016. Hallelujah--Juvenile literature. | Singers--Canada--Biography--Juvenile literature.
Classification: LCC ML3930.C5282 R3 2025 | DDC 782.42164 [B]--dc23/eng/20241009
LC record available at https://lccn.loc.gov/2024046857

Credits: End papers, Shutterstock/Cagkan Sayin; Page 32, Leonard Cohen in concert, Shutterstock/Route 66; CD Covers: *Songs of Leonard Cohen*, Columbia Records © 1967, *The Best of Leonard Cohen*, Columbia Records © 1975, and *Old Ideas*, Columbia Records © 2012.

Design by Zatar Creative
Edited by Deborah Bodin Cohen

Printed in China

9 8 7 6 5 4 3 2 1

Once there was a boy named Leonard.
He lived in Montreal, a city of cobblestones and music.

Leonard's mother sang folk songs at home in Yiddish and Russian.

On Friday nights, their house was cozy with glowing candles and challah.

Leonard's grandfather was a rabbi.

On Saturday mornings, the synagogue was so full of song, it felt like the gates of heaven were opening.

The world's beauty
made Leonard's heart sing.
In fall, leaves turned ruby red.
In summer, birds swooped and danced.

But there was sadness too—

a girl crying under a tree,

a lost little dog wandering
on the street.

Leonard wondered: How can life contain so much joy and also so much sorrow?

Was there a way to express all these feelings at once?

Leonard looked for answers.

One day, walking the cobblestone streets,
Leonard heard music weaving through the air like magic.

A man was playing a Spanish guitar—sitting on a park bench while his fingers danced on the strings.

Leonard stood there for a long time, listening.
He knew how to play guitar a little bit, but not like this!

"Can you teach me?" he asked.

The man showed Leonard how to pluck the strings. It sounded dark, like a rainy day with thunder. Leonard tried another chord: It sounded sweet as a bowl of mint chip ice cream.

The next chord buzzed like a bee nuzzling a flower. A rainbow of music flew out of his guitar. He added words: his first song!

From that day on, Leonard wrote songs about the world around him— about waking up with messy hair, about seeing a bird perched on a wire,

about drinking tea and eating oranges, friendship and love.

After a while, Leonard had enough songs for a concert.

But was he ready to play them in front of other people?

At his first concert, Leonard picked up his guitar and walked onstage. His heart beat quickly, as if it would jump out of his body.

He was so scared!

But he thought about his mother singing on Shabbat, his grandfather chanting in synagogue.

I can do this, Leonard told himself.

He took a deep breath and began to sing.

And people listened.
First a few, then a lot.

Leonard played more concerts.
Soon thousands of people
came to hear his songs!

All over the world, people
looked up at Leonard as he played,
smiling and swaying and singing along.

His music filled the whole room.
It opened people's hearts.

But there was a problem:
Leonard was missing one very special song—
a song only he could write.

He felt it inside him,
waiting to be written.
He tried and tried,
but he couldn't find the right words.
Still, he kept trying.

Leonard brought his notebook everywhere,
looking for the song.
Page after page, he scribbled—
early in the morning, late at night.

Sometimes he wanted to give up, to throw his pen and notebook away and forget the song that wanted to be sung.

But the song kept calling—

And then finally one day:
Hallelujah!

After working very hard for a very long time, Leonard finally found it:
Hallelujah!

The very last word and the very last chord. His song was done:
Hallelujah!

Leonard's song was about so many things:

How everybody makes a big mess sometimes . . . and that's okay.

How you can love someone and be mad at them at the same time. And that's okay too.

How even in the Bible, in the stories he learned from his grandfather, people were complicated.

That's just how we are.

How life is as mysterious as a secret chord:
holy, confusing, magical, and frustrating, all at once.

Leonard named his song "Hallelujah."
He couldn't wait for the world to hear it on his next album.

So no one heard Leonard's song unless he played it at a concert. And he did, night after night.

I believe in you, my song, whispered Leonard.

Then one day, a musician named Jeff heard him sing "Hallelujah" and said, "That's a song I want to sing too."

Jeff sang "Hallelujah" at his concerts, and everybody who heard it loved it.

Leonard's song began to travel the world.

People sang the song at concerts and at campfires. In synagogues and in churches. In the movies and on TV.

Alone and together.
Hallelujah, they sang, *Hallelujah!*

Now, the song that was inside Leonard's heart is inside hearts all over the world.

It's a song for all of us, deep and true, simple and complicated.

We can sing it when we need to open the gates of our own hearts.

Dear Reader,

We all have a Hallelujah inside us,

something beautiful and joyful

that we can offer the world.

Leonard's was a song.

Maybe yours is a painting, a dance,

something you bake, or something else you create.

A sport, or a story,

or your own silly jokes

that make everybody laugh.

Your Hallelujah can be anything you love.

And you can follow it forever,

wherever it leads.

Hallelujah!

Leonard Cohen (1934–2016) was a Canadian Jewish singer-songwriter, writer, and artist known for his deep soulful voice and his meaningful, poetic lyrics. Leonard explored love, loss, religion, beauty, and sadness through his music.

Leonard was born in Montreal, Quebec. He grew up in an Orthodox Jewish home and attended a Jewish day school for several years. In high school, he led the student council, acted in school theater, and learned to play guitar. He also taught himself hypnosis and tried it out on his family.

At McGill University, Leonard studied English, did poetry readings at nightclubs, and formed a country-folk band called the Buckskin Boys. Soon after graduating, he published his first book of poetry. Looking for a quiet, beautiful place to write, he lived on the Greek island of Hydra for seven years. Later, Cohen lived and wrote in a small cabin in Tennessee, complete with a horse. "That horse was mean," he once told a journalist.

In 1966, when he was thirty-two years old, Leonard moved to New York City to break into the folk music scene. After Leonard signed with Bob Dylan's manager, John Hammond, his music career grew quickly. His first of many albums, *Songs of Leonard Cohen* (1967), included instant classics like "Suzanne" and "So Long, Marianne." His first compilation album *The Best of Leonard Cohen* was released in 1975.

Leonard's most famous song, "Hallelujah," was released in 1984. It took Leonard more than ten years to finish the song, and in the process, he wrote 150 different verses, trying to find the right ones. The song grew into a sleeper hit after being covered by John Cale (1991) and Jeff Buckley (1994). "Hallelujah" gained an even wider audience when it was featured in the movie *Shrek*. Hundreds of different musicians have recorded "Hallelujah," in numerous languages, including French, Spanish, Hebrew, Arabic, Russian, Chinese, Japanese, Korean, Swedish, and Dutch.

Leonard continued to record new songs and captivate audiences worldwide into his eighties. His *Old Ideas World Tour* included 125 concerts on three continents. In 2016, Leonard released his last album. He died just three weeks later.

Leonard Cohen released 27 albums during his 52-year recording career, including these three albums released by Columbia Records in 1967, 1975, and 2012.

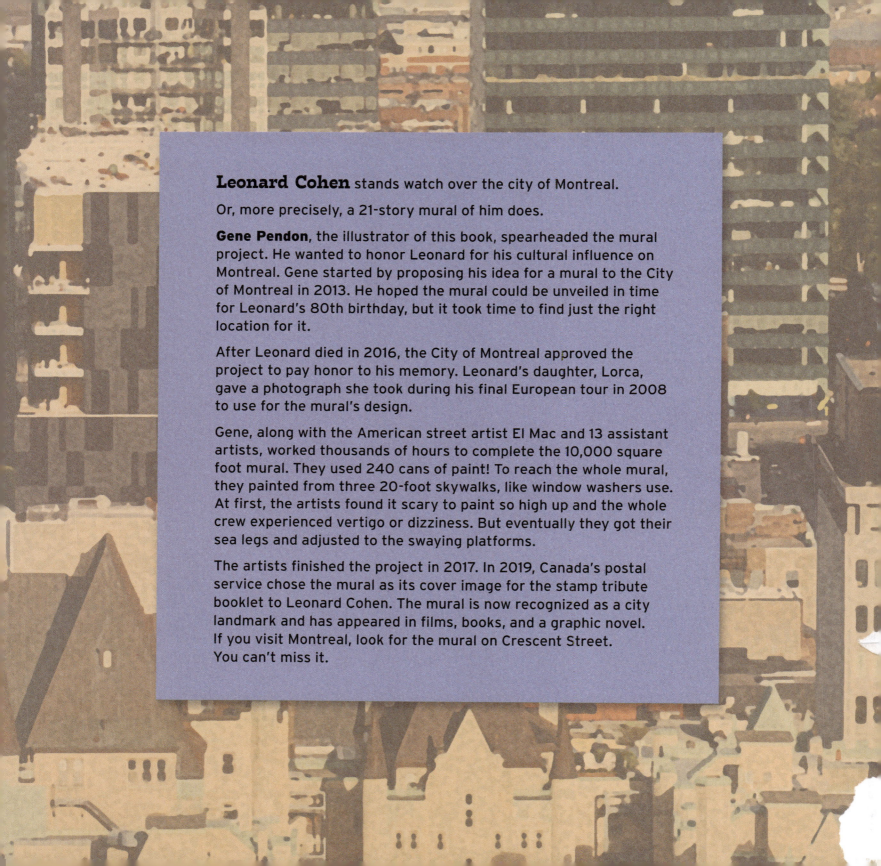

Leonard Cohen stands watch over the city of Montreal.

Or, more precisely, a 21-story mural of him does.

Gene Pendon, the illustrator of this book, spearheaded the mural project. He wanted to honor Leonard for his cultural influence on Montreal. Gene started by proposing his idea for a mural to the City of Montreal in 2013. He hoped the mural could be unveiled in time for Leonard's 80th birthday, but it took time to find just the right location for it.

After Leonard died in 2016, the City of Montreal approved the project to pay honor to his memory. Leonard's daughter, Lorca, gave a photograph she took during his final European tour in 2008 to use for the mural's design.

Gene, along with the American street artist El Mac and 13 assistant artists, worked thousands of hours to complete the 10,000 square foot mural. They used 240 cans of paint! To reach the whole mural, they painted from three 20-foot skywalks, like window washers use. At first, the artists found it scary to paint so high up and the whole crew experienced vertigo or dizziness. But eventually they got their sea legs and adjusted to the swaying platforms.

The artists finished the project in 2017. In 2019, Canada's postal service chose the mural as its cover image for the stamp tribute booklet to Leonard Cohen. The mural is now recognized as a city landmark and has appeared in films, books, and a graphic novel. If you visit Montreal, look for the mural on Crescent Street. You can't miss it.